CHANG
CHANGE YOUR LIFE

A Young Adult Guide to Fulfillment

By

Myles "The Millennial" Harris

Author's Note

Throughout the process of writing this book, I found myself learning more about life than I did before I started. Something about putting your thoughts on a page for others to receive causes you to become very vulnerable. You find yourself peeling back the layers of your memory and recognizing pivotal moments in your life that made you who you are today. Almost like peeling back the layers of an onion.

We are like an onion. We have a hard exterior that presents a certain picture to the world. However, we are nothing without the layers that help to form us. These layers grow and develop day by day and moment by moment. Our mentality is not any one layer, it is the culmination of years of experiences that have built us or deteriorated us.

I believe our purpose in life can only be found when we take the time to peel back all these layers. Diving deeper and deeper until we reveal the raw essence of our soul. The core of who we are in our most natural and vulnerable state will reveal to us how beautiful we truly are. When we consciously accept this beauty we subconsciously regain control over everybody and everything that has tried to turn us away from our truest self. They no longer have power and authority over how we view life.

We recognize that we are in control. We have the power, the motivation, and the vision to create whatever reality we desire. We have ignited an internal flame that could never be extinguished by the negativity, pain, and trauma from others. We have ultimately done the inevitable. We have become conquerors of our mentality and, in turn, have become conquerors of our life.

Change Your Mind, Change Your Life.

Table of Contents

CHAPTER 1

MENTAL FORTITUDE

"The way you see the world impacts the world you see" -Myles Harris

Growing up in the 2000s has put many of us in a space where so many outside influences are thrown into our face on a daily basis.

Now, these influences are not necessarily anything new or inherently negative. However, the issue with the current influences that impact our lives is the simple fact that they are far more covert and hidden when they are present in our lives.

We are all told the very real and present impacts of drug use, alcohol abuse, and

CHANGE YOUR MIND, CHANGE YOUR LIFE

bullying from a young age. Yet, the things that are harming our generation's mental health more than anything are oftentimes non-tangible or physical, which makes them far more scary and daunting to deal with.

One of the most pressing issues we deal with today is a condition I like to call "Perceptive Inferiority."

A condition that we develop as we grow that has no age limit, no preexisting conditions, and no outwardly present symptoms. This is a complex of sorts that we self-induce by comparing our lives to the lives of others.

Some of us are already aware of the way we can compare ourselves to others, but for many of us, diagnosing this complex is far more difficult. We do not see ourselves as individuals who always want to be like somebody else, or envious of the success of others. The reality is that this condition has far less to do with being jealous, and far more to do with self-esteem development that has been destroyed.

Have you ever found yourself looking at individuals on Instagram around your age who seem to have their life together?

They have the clothes, the money, the support, the freedom, and the LIKES. Mentally, we have become a generation that feeds more off of the perception of where somebody appears to be in life, rather than the analysis of where they actually are. We are experiencing a different inferiority complex than generations before.

In the past, for people to feel inferior to an individual, that person actually had to have more than a photo to show for it. Today, all it takes for you to feel an inner pessimism for yourself is for you to have the perception that somebody else is doing better than you based on what they selectively choose to post or express.

I have a secret for everybody reading: they are all lying.

Our mental health has been destroyed as we lack true self-confidence and self-love.

Every last one of us is struggling in our own ways. Do not allow social media to dictate your moves in your reality.

We believe the love that we are shown through social media can replace the love we have not shown ourselves in real life. We believe the love that was lacking from our parents, siblings, environment, and relationships can be supplemented if we give the perception that we are loved through an app.

This creates two types of people. One person who feels there is no hope for love for them in this world because not even social media gives them the attention they seek. Or another person who has false and empty love filling their hearts in places that need sustainable love. A rat race that chases attention and creates mental complexes that make the desire for attention govern our everyday choices.

We go from people that think, "what can I do today to make myself better and improve my growth" to people that think, "what can I do today that I can post, and how will people perceive me if I do this." Unhealthy mindsets that are creating insecure, immature, and unprepared adults.

Even in all of this, there is more than enough room to have hope. The beauty of having "Perceptive Inferiority" is that it is completely in your personal control to fix.

My remedy for healing can be summed up in a saying a close friend of mine mentioned to me many years ago: "The way you see the world impacts the world you see." A saying that states simply, however, you wake up and view this world will, in turn, become the reality of your life.

If you wake up and see the world as a place that is negative, treacherous, and against you, then your world will be one full of turmoil, uncertainty, and hate. However, if you view this world as a positive, opportunistic, and energy centered place, you will find that through time your world will become a place of happiness, spirit, and positive results.

Your mental health can be drastically improved and even transformed by making an intentional commitment to viewing situations as positive and opportunities instead of negativity and setbacks. Instead of looking to social media as a source of comparison or fulfillment, see it as a space to promote the positive changes that are taking place in your life.

Diamonds are only made under pressure. Like that diamond, only you can be molded and developed into your best self through challenges and obstacles.

Instead of continuously ranting on the negative things in your life, view these moments as challenges by the world to test your character and greet them head-on with a smile. The energy that you put into a situation is essential in determining if you grow or fold from that opportunity. Energy is the principle that our entire world flows through

Anybody who knows the Law of Conservation of Energy knows that energy can neither be created nor destroyed; energy can only be transferred or changed from one form to another.

What does this mean in terms of your mental health? It means that you are in complete control of whether you have positive or negative energy and therefore a positive or negative mindset in this world.

When we resign ourselves to the absolutes of life, we find that we can better control those battles within our power. Death, setbacks, and troubles are all absolutes in life for every person who breathes. Therefore, instead of fighting or troubling your spirit when these things occur in your life, see them as opportunities to put positive energy and positive outlook into every situation no matter how tragic the situation is.

Whatever energy you pour into the world will be manifested in your life in some other area or form.

Life, opportunity, and growth are also absolutes in life and will happen for every soul on this earth, including you. You have the power to create more life, opportunity, and growth by changing that mindset that compares your growth to others, into a mindset that focuses solely on the positive energy in your mind.

You will inherently begin to see that your world is transforming into one of light and not one of darkness. It all starts by changing your perception.

You are not inferior, you are perfectly designed and positioned to be where the world wants you to be.

Take a stand right now to view this world from a positive perspective. Be committed to this viewpoint and watch how your life changes before you even know it. "The way you see the world impacts the world you will see."

CHAPTER 2

FAITH

"As for what you cannot do...don't think you can't... think you can." -Unknown

One of the most overused and undervalued words in our society is the word "faith." We have all heard this word used thousands of times in our life. Whether it was in our religious practices or our personal life.

The problem is that this word has lost value due to a lack of explanation and application to young adults throughout our life. We are continuously told to "have faith," but nobody ever breaks down what faith truly is, and how we can identify it in our everyday life.

A simple google search defines faith as "complete trust or confidence in someone or something." The Bible defines faith as "the substance of things hoped for, the evidence of things not seen."

Both of these definitions provide vagueness as to what faith truly is and where we can find it.

Therefore, I offer a different perspective on faith. Faith is "The ability to be optimistic in seemingly pessimistic situations."

Faith is not represented and showcased in easy times. The moments when everything is going your way are not representative of the faith you hold inside. It is easy to believe and be optimistic when everything is positive.

However, it is in your spirit and mentality during tough times that your faith is truly tested. **When your back is against the wall, do you have the confidence and encouragement within your soul to continue to fight?**

Whether you are a religious individual or not, we all have faith in this world. Whether it is in the power of God, or the power of karma. All are intertwined and connected through divine energy. The beauty of being alive is that this divine energy lives within you.

Therefore when you pull on faith you are really pulling on yourself. You are encouraging and believing that all situations will come to pass because the divine energy within you will never leave you.

Nobody can take anything from you that you do not allow. Your divine energy will surround and power your days towards success and fulfillment so long as you continue to grow and water it.

Pouring into your faith simply means to pour into yourself. Walk in the belief that pessimism is a tool of evil meant to destroy your faith in yourself. When times are hard, it is mandatory for you to face that evil and tell it to leave you.

Your divine energy is stronger and more powerful than the temptation of the wicked. However, the wicked come in many shapes and forms. It is due to the disguises of evil that it is able to influence and break us down.

Evil can come in the presence of a mentally or physically abusive partner who has you imprisoned. A parent that has destroyed your self-confidence. Loss and death that can make you feel that life is unfair. The structure of society that makes you feel inferior or behind others and destroys your self-esteem.

But you need not fear evil because you express faith in just as many ways. Every time you smile when negativity is thrown your way. Every day you fight back against those who oppress you. Every time you attempt and try new opportunities without knowing the outcome. Every day you wake up and get out of bed you are literally walking in faith. This life is unpredictable and if you didn't believe in yourself, you wouldn't be alive.

You win every day you try.

Martin Luther King Jr. stated, "Faith is taking the first step even when you don't see the whole staircase."

We will never be able to know what the future holds. Therefore don't allow pessimism and negativity about your future hold you back from achieving in the present. We spend our days as young adults today worrying about tomorrow. Where we will be in five years, or thirty. Life is so unpredictable and we allow that fear of the unknown to control our every move.

This breeds anxiety from self-imposed factors. Our self-esteem is lowered and we cause ourselves to live in fear over faith mindset.

These forces within you will cause your inner me to become your enemy. Destroying you from the inside out and making you feel lost when you are the navigator in control of your destiny the entire trip.

You have to break free of these pessimistic mindsets and operate in optimism. Because optimism is truly the only logical way to live. Positive energy is the only reasonable energy that we can use that can plant seeds, water, and then grow them.

When the enemy tries to shoot you down, meet them with a smile. When people laugh at your dreams, turn it into motivation to go harder. When you second guess yourself, remember that your mind is the only thing that can truly hold you back.

You are powerful beyond measure. You have powers you never dreamed of. You can do things you never thought you could do. **There are no limitations as to what you can do, besides the limitations of your own mind.** As for what you cannot do, don't think you can't, think you can.

Calm down and take the time to believe in yourself, because you are worth it. Reassure your mind that everything will work in your favor. Have faith in who you were uniquely called to be. Seek approval from no one but the divine energy that runs through your body.

You can call on this energy whenever you please. It is yours. You control your path. You control your destiny. No matter what cards life has dealt you, play another hand. It's only 4 aces in the deck, and they are yours for the taking. Bet on yourself until you can't bet anymore, and then bet on yourself again.

This mindset never stops, because your faith will never stop. It will never leave you nor forsake you.

You have every mindset within you that it takes to win. All that matters is if you are willing to shift your perspective in order to move faith first instead of fear first.

BET ON YOU.

CHAPTER 3

DATING

"Dating is like an airport, everybody comes with baggage" -Myles Harris

Dating in this day and age is completely screwed. There, I said it. There is no hope for any of us out here to find love and have successful relationships. We are doomed to the cycle of toxic behavior and temporary love forever. So, please skip this chapter now because I have no hope or wisdom to give you!

Ok. Now that I have your attention. I want you to realize that everything I just said is completely true. I also want you to realize that every last outcome is within your control. These toxic traits and piss-poor outcomes we all have experienced are very real outcomes in today's world. Most of us, sadly, are carrying the mindsets that manifest these negative outcomes. Our exposure to the world has set us up for failure and we must unwrap the quirks that have damaged our perception on how a successful relationship can be built and sustained. There are 3 main subjects we must conquer first.

The first topic at hand, ironically, is not what we have been exposed to. It is actually what we have not been exposed to; representation. By representation, I mean that many of us did not have an example of a successful relationship within our households growing up. The American Psychological Association reports that 40-50% of marriages end in divorce.

Divorces are more than just legal separation of income and property. They are emotional and mental earthquakes that can shake individuals to their core. Sadly, kids often are the most affected by the aftermath of divorces. Seeing the two people who pledged their life and love to each other split can confuse a child. Leaving many children to wonder how they themselves could find love when the people who brought them into this world could not make it work.

If we add in the number of marriages that never ended in a legal divorce but with an eternal emotional separation, we are left with little hope. **More than half of the people you interact with come from unconventional households that have without a doubt shaped them into the person they are today.**

Seeing success is a pivotal factor in believing in yourself to be able to succeed as well. Children pick up many of the characteristics shown by their parents. When they were not able to display success, we are left lost and moving aimlessly with our hearts exposed in the wrong places. While there is no such thing as a perfect relationship, having a healthy representation of lifelong love and commitment can provide a young adult with a resource to turn to for guidance and wisdom. It becomes difficult when you are trying to conquer love, and the people you love most can only tell you what not to do, rather than what to do. They only learned from their mistakes, but they never got to learn from success.

If you come from an unhealthy parental relationship, the key is to seek mentorship. Find the representation that can provide you with guidance on how to better yourself for a successful mindset. We all have that friend whose parents have a seemingly perfect relationship and have been dating for decades. Or the older couple that lives up the street with more wisdom than we could absorb in a lifetime. Utilize these individuals as a source of solace and comfort. **Their knowledge can give you hope and confidence that you can succeed where your parents could not.**

We must remember the old idiom, "you cannot be what you cannot see." When trauma, separation, and failure has been the main outcomes of the relationships around you, dating can seem a horrific and daunting task. Utilize the wisdom that is available and pursue the guidance of a successful couple. This investment in you will pay off for generations to come, literally.

The second issue we are facing in our generation is a hypersexualized culture that is deteriorating our mind and soul. Before our eyes, we have become a society where sex is the focus of the majority of pop culture in one form or another. Our media platforms push sex as a way to express freedom and happiness. Many of our generation's "celebrities" lack any form of talent or work ethic, but gain notoriety for doing a basic task with exceptional physiques.

Men and women alike are capitalizing on a world that has manipulated us into thinking that sharing ourselves with anyone we please is an empowering characteristic. We have lost a moral standard as a society. **Us as young adults need to realize that just because you**

could, doesn't mean you should. Everything that you could do is not something you should do.

There are consequences to all our actions and we need to understand that sex is one of our most intimate forms of expression. It is something that we are supposed to hold close and dear and share it with those we have carefully picked. However, men are pushed to lose their virginities at insanely unprepared ages by any means necessary. Simply to feel fulfilled as a man. Women have been pushed to believe that sexual promiscuity equals spiritual freedom.

In reality, both of these actions lead us down paths of darkness and clouds that we can only cover up with more sex and trauma. **We are giving our intimate energy to a bad receptor. This will always cause spiritual distortion, spiritual disruption, and spiritual confusion.**

We have to understand that the sexual energy that flows through our bodies at our young age is a powerful tool.

Feeding into this hypersexualized culture has made us put short term pleasures over long term progress. We have tricked our minds into thinking that these actions are "just fun." When we have sex, there is an exchange of energies that takes place. This is the reason oftentimes emotional attachment follows because sex was never meant to be recreational.

Our bodies are designed to hold sex at a primal level of importance that is connected to the rest of our body. **We are failing at dating because many of us are giving the most intimate side of ourselves up for fun and expecting feelings in return.**

We are working in opposition to our body's design. Intimacy must be experienced without the use of sex if we wish to improve our chances of success. Do not allow this oversexualized culture to brainwash you any further. Your actions are destroying you.

Lastly, we suck at dating because we need a reality check. News flash for everyone reading: relationships are hard. I have another news flash for everyone: you cannot succeed if you give up. These two are realities that you must accept and realize before and during the dating process. Many of us do not want to accept these realities because it goes against the status quo we live by. Comfort over compromise.

We have been pushed into a very entitled and self-serving mindset. One where if things are not the way you like them, just leave. We are told to be independent and "just do you" so often that we have lost the will to persevere through struggles.

A relationship is an imperfect bond between two imperfect people. Realize that and embrace it. Do not run away from somebody who challenges you and the way you think. Do not leave someone simply because you are going through a tough time in the relationship.

The reality of love is that relationships are not 50/50.

They are 100/100. 100% of your effort and your partner's effort is required to make this thing work.

There will be moments where one of you is not able to give their full energy. You and your partner must have trust and understanding that it is the obligation of the other partner to pick up the slack.

"The key to a successful relationship is not finding the right person, it's about loving the person you found." -Anonymous

Society has twisted our minds so much that we believe staying with someone during hard times makes us weak.

I argue that there is nothing more admirable and strong than sticking with something you believe in despite adversity.

Our emotions have been hijacked to make us feel inferior if things are not successful. That someone must know how to love us perfectly. A person learns how to love you minute by minute, day by day, and year by year.

Perfection does not exist in this world and you will be hurt by the people you love. However, you need not fear or run away from pain. The key is to analyze and decipher what pain is and is not worth it.

I have a saying, "dating is like an airport, everybody comes with baggage."

You are not perfect and you have harmed people in your life with your words or actions. Naturally, people will harm you as well. Whether these actions are intentional or not does not change the fact that they will come inevitably in your relationships. There will come a time where you and your partner will be tested to your core on how bad you want your partnership to work. It will require you to put compromise over comfort. There will be many new and foreign things you will have to adapt to.

If this sounds like something you are adverse to then you are not prepared for what it takes to make a relationship work. Save the other person some time and focus on preparing your mind to sacrifice for another person's happiness.

Until you can commit to being a person that will address your own flaws and insecurities with your partner, the relationship will not work.

Until you can allow yourself to be completely vulnerable to the person you love, the relationship will not work.

Choose wisely the person you call your partner. They can either build you to new heights or cause your world to come tumbling down.

A relationship is an investment. All investments take time, effort, and patience. There will be many ups and many downs in this investment. If you choose the right person, however, the reward will far outweigh the cost.

Nuri Muhammad said, "The most important decision you will ever make in your life after choosing your spiritual path, is the mate you choose to spend the rest of your life with. They will either inspire you to grow into your greatness or they will confine you to complacency. They will either be your other half, or they will make you half of yourself."

Relationships were never meant to be comfortable. They were never meant to be easy or be perfect when you meet the "right person." Any two people can be right if they are willing to work and sacrifice for success. As J. Cole said, "there is beauty in the struggle."

Change your mindset to be prepared to go to war with your partner. Remember that you are never fighting at each other but fighting for each other. You are on the same team.

There will be many storms but remember this one saying: "Life isn't about waiting for the storm to pass. It's about learning how to dance in the rain." -Vivian Greene

CHAPTER 4

MOVING WITH INTENTION

"Intentional living is the art of making our own choices before others' choices make us"- Richie Norton

Waking up with no purpose is the number one killer of dreams.

We should never underestimate the power that the first 5 minutes of our day have. During that time, we develop and set the tone for the remainder of our day. In those moments we either set ourselves up for progression or for regression. Anything in between is unacceptable.

How do you wake up? Do you sit in a groggy state that is constantly thinking about how you would much rather sleep?

We find this to be a harmless behavior that does not negatively affect us once we wake up and get started on our day. However, that mindset is completely false and backward.

Take a second to think about the state you are willingly choosing to stay in. You are in a mindset that is living in the past rather than focusing on the present. Wishing to be sleep when you are blessed to be awake. Regretting prior opportunities instead of loving future possibilities. Dreading the fact that you are awake and in the open spirit of having life.

This is where we first lose our sight on the importance of moving with intention. Have you ever been hurt by somebody and when they apologized for their actions they said, "My intentions were never to hurt you?" When a person has no intent, they do not mean to do anything. Their actions and outcomes were not the preplanned results they had anticipated. They lacked control and forethought. Regardless of their intention, they still hurt you. Not intending to do harm does not erase the fact that every action has consequences. That pain is still very present, and now you and that person are left to deal with the scars of their lack of intent.

Your mind when it is moving without intention is similar to this scenario. It moves through the day without a purpose and perspective for what the bigger picture is and how it affects your success. Leaving you needlessly bumping your head and leaving wounds and scars that could have been avoided.

Moving with intention is a frame of mind that simply means "to take control." Consequences can be good or bad. **However, when you move with intent you will inevitably put yourself in a better position to make sure more of those consequences are positive rather than negative.**

Taking control over your thoughts even in those first 5 minutes is a key step to set you up for success in the coming day. If the first thing you look at is the messages on your phone, or your social media platforms you are already losing control. Now, the control of your mood and mental state is up to how other people's messages and posts make you feel. If you encounter drama, death, or mindless content you have allowed negativity to be the first energy consumed into your body.

You can take control of your first energy and thoughts through a few different actions. You can use that same cellular device to play positive or spiritual music that makes you feel sufficient. Having personal time in a positive state to start your day will have you maneuvering with a smile on your face rather than a frown.

You can view or listen to mental podcasts, interviews, or shows that feed your brain with information that is vital to your spirit. Motivational speakers, artists, and influencers that empower you to be your best self can give you the strength to take on the world.

Go through your day with one mindset: Win the day.

I did not say win the week, the month, or the year. Win the day. Too many times we make unrealistic outlooks that are too big for our mind to process.

It is the small steps you take every single day that creates the outcome for your week, year, and life.

Therefore you must start by winning the day.

Will this be easy? No.

Will you lose the day sometimes? Yes.

Will it be worth it? Absolutely.

If you are unwilling to put in the work, you have to settle for the fact that you are going to fall short of where you want to be.

Mediocrity will become your reality. That is one guarantee in a world full of unknowns.

It starts from that first breath you take in the morning. You have to not only be able to think your steps, you have to put your feet to work to make them real.

Manifestation without movement is meaningless.

One last step you can take is to be in a sedentary state that has intention. This can be through meditation, prayer, or simple positive affirmation.

How do these differ from when you wake up and think about being sleep? The difference comes from the fact that you are not thinking of mindless subjects that no longer matter. In mediation, prayer, or affirmations, your thoughts and actions are centered on processing and centering your spiritual, mental, and physical being. These different tips all move with intention and give you control over the energy inside of your being.

Of course, you cannot control everything in your life that happens. Things arise throughout our everyday life that can bring us down, or distract us from the goals we had in mind. However, when you are moving with intention, it is far harder for the enemy to break you.

Yes, the enemy can distract you with things they know have controlled you. Substance addictions, gossip, finances, lust, and family issues are all blockers to your goals. Nobody is perfect, and make no mistake you will lose to some of these influences from time to time in your life. When you move with intention, you are able to minimize the consequences of those obstacles when they form in your life.

Remember the social media trend, "Would you rather cry in a Nissan or a Phantom." While it is horribly toxic in nature, there is a great correlation to our personal life. There will be times you will not complete all your goals or experience setbacks. You will struggle and be put down by others on your journey to fulfillment. But because you have been walking with intention, those negative blockers are not able to break you.

MYLES "THE MILLENNIAL" HARRIS

Yes, you may have not have gotten the result you wanted, but because you have been taking intentional steps to make connections and working hard you still are far beyond where others are. It's one thing to be down. It's a whole other thing to be down and out.

Keep in mind that nobody is positive 100% of the time. **We are not trying to seek perfection in life, only promotion. Perfection is the enemy of progress.**

Your objective is to move through life doing the correct things most people won't so that you can have what most people never will: fulfillment. This is a long and hard road to success but you need not to bat an eye. The race is not given to the swift nor the strong but he who endures to the end.

Once you wake up and have focused your energy into a positive space, you must find your purpose for the day. Without a purpose, you cannot have intention, and therefore no promise.

It would be similar to driving a car with a blindfold on, you have no sense of direction. Intention requires direction for it to be applied correctly. How do you find this purpose and direction? You must plan.

Take the time to think out the mandatory things you need to accomplish and assign time to them. Whether virtually in a calendar or on a physical planner, you must have a tangible to-do list that can lift most of the burden off of you. Account time for the smallest of tasks, whether it is calling your family, or leaving personal time to refresh. Removing guesswork removes excuses.

Excuses are the number one enemy of a man or woman on a mission. They give you superficial and false reasoning as to why something cannot be done, rather than giving you the motivation to see your mission through to completion.

The use of excuses will leave you in a desolate and dark space of nothingness. You will remain stagnant and find yourself in a rat race as to why you cannot better your own situation.

The irony is when those excuses influence you to fail and you are trying to self-analyze why things happen, you will then side with more excuses. Never accepting personal accountability. Never taking control. Intention is the key.

At the end of the day, you will either be able to reflect and be proud of the steps you took for progression, or you will be disappointed.

How can you be ok being mediocre when it comes to your life and your future? Why waste another damn day of your life asking questions when it is your responsibility to go find the answers. Bad things will happen to us all, but that is no excuse to give up.

It is through your intentional actions that you will find success and be proud of who you are. Every step you take must have intent behind it. **The way you walk must carry a**

presence of confidence and security that you know who you are, even if you don't.

By believing you can accomplish extraordinary feats you make yourself your own superhero. You took control and saved your own life which will allow you to save others. The beauty of moving with intention is that it will eventually become natural, and once it becomes natural you are the most lethal weapon on the planet.

"Excuses are tools of the incompetent, used by those to build monuments of nothingness, and those who use them seldom amount to anything."

Either you will be nothing in this world or you will be something. That outcome is completely up to you.

It doesn't matter what living situation you came from, you must take the steps now to change it for the future. It doesn't matter your financial or mental situation, it is up to you to reframe your mind to take control of those areas of your life. Stop allowing the world to control you. Intention is a two-way street and either it happens to you, or you happen to it.

As Richie Norton said, "Intentional living is the art of making our own choices before others' choices make us."

Take control.

CHAPTER 5

LEADERSHIP

"Humility is not thinking less of yourself, it's thinking of yourself less." · CS Lewis

Leadership in and of itself has a major misconception. It is surrounded in an aura that is grandiose. We celebrate the positions we win, the promotions at our jobs, or milestones in our business ventures. And through those celebrations, we assign value to our life.

Leadership has become a title and a fallacy, rather than a job and a position of love.

When we think of leaders we think of the rank that they have over others. "President," "CEO," "Supervisor," all have connotations that relate to being superior or higher than others.

The mistake that most organizations and institutions make when choosing "leader" leadership is actually believing the hype surrounding the title.

A true leader operates not from experience or position. Nor from superiority or assured ness. Not from self-confidence or ego. A true leader operates from the core of their humanity: their heart.

While it may seem cliché, I promise that the reason so many groups fail, or can never exceed prior results is almost always due to poor leadership. Many times these people who are called leaders have no heart, and therefore are no leader at all.

Leadership is not a position of glamour, it is a position of service. Leadership is a dirty job, with dirty hands, and dirty hours. It takes humility and empathy. **You cannot lead if you cannot follow. If you cannot place yourself in**

the shoes of every person you serve, you are already ill-equipped to lead.

Understand that leadership is not a role nor a title. Leadership is shown through the heart of every individual in the moments when it is easy to turn a blind eye. Whether you have the title of CEO or intern, you have the power to lead. All it takes is heart.

Servant leadership is crucial to the success of any leader and those they serve. When you, as a leader, can show that you are not higher, but actually lower than those you work with, you will experience a change like no other. When you do the small things everybody overlooks, you inevitably motivate those around you to adopt the same outlook.

Nobody can be what they cannot see for themselves. Therefore, if you want your company to have a spirit of excellence, the leader must showcase a spirit of excellence.

This is not shown through company statements and fancy public relations stunts. It is shown through the day to day interactions when you think nobody is watching. **The way you do anything is the way you do everything.**

Cultivate a spirit within yourself to be personable with every soul that walks this earth. If you feel anybody is beneath you, then nobody will ever support you being above them. From the highest ranking official you meet to the lowest paying janitor. Serve them all the same. From the richest investor you meet to the homeless man on the side of the street you pass daily, serve them all the same.

Understand that people all operate off of different frequencies, and therefore, we all possess different leadership styles. You must understand the person you are first, to then understand your style of leadership.

Some people are extroverts, and therefore extroverted leaders. They are very ambitious and courageous go-getters, who like to get moving on things as soon as possible. They see value in trying new things and learning as they go. They move quickly and effectively and believe that through hard work they will achieve successful results.

Some people are introverts, and therefore introverted leaders. They are very mild-mannered and wise and see value in patience. They are often cerebral and cunning planners, who can mastermind any opportunity. They see value in taking a step back and listening so they can read the thoughts of the room before they make a decision. They believe through intellectual thought and patience they will be able to work smart, not hard.

Some people feel they don't fall in either category. They do not see themselves as a leader. They care not for positions or to have others look to them for guidance. They see value in personal growth and personal evaluation. The amazing thing is, while they don't know it, they are tremendous leaders as well.

Leadership has no one size fits all mentality. Different strokes for different folks is the name of the game. However, never fall into the trap of believing that you are not "fit" to be a leader.

This is a societal construct that has left millions to lead average lives because they see themselves as different. There is only one mandatory thing you must have to be a leader. No magical characteristic, shiny clothes, or speaking skills. The only thing you must have to be a leader is heart.

Your heart is the key to all leadership, not the position. When you cultivate that true selfless spirit, you will see how natural blessings will begin to come your way. **But remember, if the end goal is to receive blessings rather than to give them, you will never win in the long run.**

Being in a leadership position will expose your heart. You will be faced with many opportunities and choices. Choices to let others clean up the event, and you go home because that "isn't your job." Or to serve alongside those cleaning and volunteer your help. Choices to let that piece of trash stay on the ground that you shot towards the trash can, or turn around and take the time to pick it up.

Your actions are a manifestation of the person you are on the inside. While we are not perfect, we can work to follow our hearts and do the right thing.

Mark Miller states in his bestseller, "The Heart of Leadership," that in order to have the heart of a leader you must "Think others first." It is only through love and selflessness that true successful leadership can be accomplished.

Make no mistake, this journey will be difficult. It is challenging to check your natural thoughts of what will benefit your life in the heat of the moment. There is pain in rejecting temporary shine for a dimmer task that must be accomplished away from the cameras. But your heart will be unmatched, and that will make you different from everyone else.

Being a leader requires you to sacrifice many of the aspects of ourselves that we have developed to protect ourselves.

Everything is your fault. Things will be unfair and you will have to be chastised for things that many times were not your responsibility in the first place.

People will criticize when they are in no position to reprimand you. The reality is, as a leader, you have to learn how to take all of this in stride. You cannot become emotional in the face of criticism because there is a bigger picture and a bigger group you represent other than yourself.

These people are looking to you for guidance and if you lose your cool in uncomfortable times, what do you expect everyone else to do?

The expectations you set through your actions will be the standards they will hold themselves accountable to. Provide the tools for everyone else to win by showcasing in your everyday demeanor how they should operate.

Every decision, reaction, and move must be made for the wellbeing of others. That is true leadership.

CS Lewis states, "Humility is not thinking less of yourself, it's thinking of yourself less." Only by manifesting a thought process and changing our mind to "think others first," can we then change our life as leaders.

There are no shortcuts to servant leadership. There are no shortcuts to success. There are no elevators, you must take the stairs.

CHAPTER 6

FRIENDSHIP

"Show me your friends and I'll show you
who you are" -Grandma

One of the foundational elements of life is companionship. This concept of another being that you can share experiences, thoughts, and emotions with. We see these in the form of a romantic partner, a pet, a sibling, or even bigger: a friend.

You see, friendship is a concept with positive connotations because it helps to ease our fears. Our internal fears of loneliness and abandonment violate our existence as social creatures. Therefore, we seek others to bring a sense of worth and peace to our life by making friends. People who you can laugh, smile, and enjoy great times with help to make life worth living.

However, I would argue that what we should be fearing is not abandonment and loneliness. **Our true fear should be companionship in the company of individuals who offer no opportunity for growth in our lives.**

The company you keep will become you. And many times, in our young adult life, we have our values when it comes to friends out of place with our position in life. We want to be leaders, yet we hang around followers. We want to be wealthy, yet we hang around poor minded people. We want to be successful, yet we hang around individuals who are comfortable with mediocrity.

To place yourself in an incorrect company for your position in life is to dance with the devil. When we are in an unhealthy friendship dynamic, we find ourselves trading in loneliness and getting failure in return. Yes, you receive the happy times and the sense of belonging. But to belong to a group of mediocrity is to limit your own light.

Friendship is never supposed to be a burden or obstacle in your dreams to life. Friendship is designed to be a catalyst to provide support, motivation, and preparation for the challenges of the world.

Too many times we find ourselves in groups that drain us of our happiness. We consistently find ourselves involved in unnecessary and negative situations that inevitably tear us down. Even the strongest house can become weakened if it is hit enough from the inside.

To allow somebody to receive the title of friend is to place them in a position to see your vulnerabilities. This is not something any person should take lightly. If this position is given to the wrong group, you will find yourself deteriorated and lost.

You have allowed the wrong person to enter into a space in your heart and mind

CHANGE YOUR MIND, CHANGE YOUR LIFE

where they now have the power to affect your energy. You have given them the keys to the car, which is your spirit, and they can send you into a head-on collision with failure.

It is crucial on your journey to fulfillment to surround yourself with individuals who are able to challenge you out of love. **Your circle should be composed of people who have their own individual ambitions and are all working together to achieve them.**

Symbiotic relationships have always created great opportunities and unimaginable outcomes. Whether this group is 1 person or 10 people. Everybody must know the mission and everybody must be committed to its purpose.

A friend group of "yes men" and "yes women" will lead you to a lifetime of no's from all the wrong people. You will find yourself believing you are right because the people around you have not challenged your thought processes and actions. You will continuously find yourself being rejected and dealing with no's when the pivotal moments in your life arise because your condition was never elevated.

Friendship should be rooted in principle and built through experiences. If your circle has principles that align with every individual's dreams then you have the opportunity to achieve great things. Holding values such as unrelenting support, accountability, and success can enable everyone to live their best life.

No individual is self-made. We all require support and help throughout our life to gain knowledge and answers where we can't seem to find them. A friend is able to help you find those answers without belittling you in the process. They show support and love simply because they love you and want you to win.

Beware of those who walk in when you shine and leave when situations are uncomfortable for them.

They are not the passengers ready for the bumpy road that is your journey to fulfillment.

They say you are the average of the 5 people you spend the most time with. The power of attraction and environment are very real and have serious effects on our life. Have you ever noticed that in an uncomfortable and negative environment, you inevitably feel that negative energy spill onto you overtime? No matter how hard you try to fight it, it does become very evident in your life in different ways.

The same can be said for positive environments. No matter how negative or down your soul may be, that positive energy continues to radiate around you until it becomes you.

Their thoughts will start to become your thoughts. Their actions will start to become your actions. One way or another you will succumb to the circumstances of your environment. It is your decision whether your friend group is going to provide a healthy environment or a detrimental environment. If you play around with fire long enough, you will one day get burnt. However, there is no fire in your environment to burn yourself on, then you have maneuvered around an unnecessary obstacle on your pathway to success.

Your friends can either be the negative energy that will deteriorate your hopes and dreams. Or your friends will be the positive light necessary to propel you through good and bad times so that you can reach heights you never thought possible.

If you find yourself always being the smartest person in the group, that is a sign that you need to level up. That circle does not offer the enlightenment that you require in order to improve upon the individual you are today.

If you find that your friend group spends more time talking about other people and their problems than they spend speaking on their own issues, run. Anybody who can constantly degrade and talk down on other people for their shortcomings is lacking the love and energy you need to manifest into your best self.

You cannot grow if you are too busy applying your energy and attention to things that do not matter.

We all will fall short at times. Be careful when you have a friend group that is quick to point a finger at others, but never realize they have 4 fingers pointing back at them.

If the conversation is not uplifting and empowering, leave it alone. Rid yourselves of those individuals as they hold negativity in their hearts. Their heart will become yours the longer you stay around it. Messy people create a mess that you will one day have to clean up.

Another way to identify an unhealthy friendship is to simply take a step back and look at your group. Ask yourself, do you find yourself inspired by the individuals in front of you? Do they make you feel a sense of greatness and excitement about your future? And most importantly, do you believe they are the group that can support you unselfishly on your different successes and failures in life?

If the answer to any of those questions is no, then it is time to move forward in another direction. Your time on earth is limited and your future success is nothing to trifle with. **The energy and actions of those around us, directly and indirectly, affect our success.** You become the environment that you surround yourself in.

There can be no loose ends when you are on a mission for your life. This journey will be long, rough, and rugged. But happy are those who dream dreams and are willing to pay the price to make those dreams come true. Ask yourself, are your friends willing to pay the price for those dreams as well? Sacrifice, pain, love, and happiness will be required. So choose wisely.

Ask yourself "who am I?" And you will find the answer as to who your friends must be. Or better yet, show me your friends, and I will show you who you are.

Chapter 7

WEALTH

"The real measure of wealth is how much you'd be worth if you lost it" -Benjamin Jowett

Everything we have been taught about money from a traditional standpoint is a lie. A lie that has been continuously perpetuated to leave us in a rat race where we are fighting for our next check, and never truly living.

We believe that wealth is achieved once we reach a certain dollar amount in our account. Or we believe we are rich when we secure that six or seven-figure salary. However, this very concept is a lie.

The truth that nobody tells us about money and wealth is that money means nothing. And therefore, the chasing of nothing will inevitably lead you to a state of emptiness. Money has no intrinsic value. That is, money in and of itself is simply a piece of paper.

The only value it truly holds is between the two people who believe it to represent something more than what it truly is: nothing. It is in this pursuit of money that we lose touch with the reality of what is truly valuable in life.

Am I saying that money serves no purpose and we should never be wise with it? No

What I am saying is that money is only valuable for one reason, and that is to afford us time.

J. Cole rapped, "They say time is money, but really it's not. If we ever go broke, time is all we got."

Time is the only thing that holds true value because it is finite. It cannot be recreated and handed to any individual just because they ask for it or work for it. We are all on a ticking clock waiting for the day it strikes midnight on our life.

Therefore, to be in pursuit of a dollar amount is to be foolish. To be in pursuit of time is to be wise.

The wealthiest minds on earth have all come to a place of realization that money can be made and lost by the millions and billions every day. It is printed, transacted, torn, and burned on the daily and yet we spend our entire lives chasing it. It is because we are so focused on the money itself that we live our whole lives and never utilize what money grants us in time.

As you achieve more financial growth the goal is to buy yourself more time. More time with your family because you have to spend less time working. More time traveling and seeing the world because your business is on autopilot.

These are the things that make money valuable. A wealthy person has the freedom of time on their side. They no longer are in the race to maximize their profits but have shifted their focus into maximizing their time.

If you wish to achieve more wealth and accumulate more time, you must first start by devaluing the importance of money in your life.

It sounds ironic that the way to make more money is to actually care about money less. However, the reality is much simpler than what we were ever taught.

Wealth will require you to take chances and be open to different avenues of opportunity. It will demand you to be contented, hardworking, and patient as you push towards your financial goals. If you do not decrease the value of money in your mind, you will always be pressed for more.

Your mindset will surround making money just to make money, rather than making money to have more time. You will never reach a number that satisfies you, and because you placed all your value in that number you are empty.

We live our entire lives as consumers, and therefore, we think as consumers do. Constantly, looking for what to buy and where to spend our money. Never stopping to think about how we can grow and multiply our wealth.

A consumer-minded individual is a slave to the mindset and desires of the masses. Popularity determines the things they wish to buy. All to fit a mold that their social group has painted as superior.

Our lack of financial literacy allows money to have too much control over us. We spend our last dime to buy things that make us feel better because we are accepted. Then complain about constantly remaining broke. This is a recipe for disaster and young adults are the biggest victims of this.

Nuri Muhammad said that the main issue with us and money is within our mindset. "We buy things we don't need, with money we don't have, from people we don't like, to impress people we don't know."

We have a lot of dollars, but we need more sense.

You are lost because a number defined your worth on this earth.

Let go of how important riches are and you will immediately become more valuable. Your mindset will open doors to other sources of income you never thought possible. Your perspective will treat money as a tool to fulfillment rather than the end goal of success.

Your hourly rate, salary, business contract, and sales do not determine your success. Success is determined by your inner soul reflecting on the freedom you have to use your time wisely. So long as you are confined and controlled by money, you will never be free.

A billion dollars could fall in your lap and you would be the poorest person in the world because you never understood how little money actually means.

Any Rand stated, "Money is only a tool. It will take you wherever you wish, but it will not replace you as a driver." You control the path your life will take.

If you choose to continuously chase money, you will find it right alongside your troubles. However, if you take advantage of time, wealth will be a byproduct that will fulfill you.

This journey for spiritual wealth and financial freedom will require you to surround yourself with like-minded individuals. A lion cannot run around in a cage and believe it will become king of the jungle. It will only become the king of the zoo.

The individuals you surround yourself with must be driven on their purpose and promise, not profits. Pursuing your purpose will grant you happiness and fulfillment on levels few will ever experience. Your circle of friends must have this same vision for their own lives.

Ask yourself what your time is invested in? Is it surrounded and utilized by purpose-driven people or profit-driven people?

Redefine the goal of your relationships and life in order to align your spirit with true prosperity.

Is your partner a worthy investment? We must analyze the most intimate relationships we maintain as this is where our heart and mind applies the most energy. **The smartest investment a person can make in life is into a partner who believes in their purpose.**

When you have a partner with a wealthy mind, money will never be the problem or the solution. It will simply be a tool to afford you both time and experience.

Wealthy mindsets recognize the insignificance of a dollar and rather chase the fulfillment of their dreams and happiness. Taking advantage and reclaiming the time you have on earth to use every day chasing fulfillment will always be a worthy effort.

Ask yourself, are you chasing finances, or are you chasing fulfillment? One will leave you empty and addicted time and time again. The other will give you eternal peace and happiness.

Follow your heart, not the money. My father always told me, "I have never seen a Brinks truck following a hearse." You cannot take it with you beyond the grave. So live in the now by letting go of worldly desires for wealth.

Then and only then will you be able to take advantage of the time you have and maximize both your purpose and your profits.

Invest in your mindset before you seek to invest your money. Invest in your friends before you invest in your finances. Invest in your partner before you invest in profits.

Doing the latter first will leave you stuck. You will make money and come across opportunities plenty of times throughout your life. It's the mentality you have that will bring you to a place of true wealth, peace, and fulfillment.

One day that money will leave you and what will you have to show for it? Wealth is not defined in the number of zeroes on your tax return. Or by the luxurious items you own.

But rather, "the real measure of wealth is how much you'd be worth if you lost it."

CHAPTER 8

WISDOM

"The fool doth think he is wise, but a wise man knows himself to be a fool"- William Shakespeare

In life, we are destined to make mistakes. We will fumble the ball, trip, and fall, and knock ourselves out more times than we count. From relationships to money and everything in between. We will not be perfect.

Yet we all seek to become better and learn from those mishaps. We want to perfect our wrongdoings and never bump our heads again. We believe that knowledge is gained only through experience, and therefore, it is mandatory for us to bump our heads in order to learn.

However, there comes a time in life where we must seek to be wise instead of smart.

While the two seem to go hand and hand, there is one major difference in their application.

You see, a smart individual makes a mistake and then learns from it and does not repeat it. A wise individual, on the other hand, watches the mistake the smart person made and avoids it in their life altogether.

As you grow older, you begin to realize certain lessons are not worth the punishment and consequences of experiencing them.

When we were younger, many of us were the children who did the exact opposite of what our parents told us.

We were told not to put our hand on the stove because it was too hot, and yet we still had to be burned to believe it. We had to experience it ourselves to become a believer in its existence and truth.

This is detrimental when you are on your path to fulfillment. When you have the opportunity to avoid certain obstacles by learning from the mistakes of others you would be wise to listen. As we grow older the consequences are no longer temporary and minuscule.

Time out has turned into prison. No allowance has turned into financial failure. Flirtatious friends and crushes have turned into broken hearts and spiritual toxicity. All of the consequences of life elevate as you elevate.

As you grow, so do the problems and challenges of the world. **One of the keys to exercising wisdom is to learn from the mistakes of others. Where they took a left turn and things went downhill, you need to go right.**

The examples of failure and success are before our eyes every day. It is simply up to us to open our vision and choose to apply what we are seeing.

Many of us live for the thrill of trying everything out. Tasting the rainbow of life's challenges to see which ones we like and don't like. However, there is a major flaw in this thinking.

Some consequences from tasting the rainbow remain on your tongue a lot longer than necessary.

Certain mistakes can become cancer. A virus and unwanted energy in your body that destroys you from the inside out because that consequence stays with you.

The reality is that it likely could have been avoided by exercising wisdom.

I am in no way encouraging you to live a boring life, but I am empowering you to know what consequences you can and cannot live with. Understand that these consequences can take a life of their own and become bigger than you ever imagined.

You can choose the crime, but you cannot choose the punishment.

There is an old saying that the more things change, the more they stay the same. This saying reveals that no matter how rapidly our world flips, grows, and turns, there will always be certain inevitable truths to life. These truths remain the same through generations and centuries. They are not subject to time and therefore if we can learn them without experiencing them we have an advantage.

Wisdom gives you the advantage of avoiding consequences that can alter and setback the manifestation of your life. When trusted individuals warn you of the path you are headed down, take heed to what they say. The game does not change, only the players and the teams.

Their experience and failure will become your wisdom and success if you choose to value and apply them.

William Shakespeare once wrote, "The fool doth think he is a wise man, but the wise man knows himself to be a fool."

This contradicting statement of this reveals another key to what wisdom truly is and how we can obtain it.

When you understand that wisdom is simply certain truths about life that never change, you begin to realize that there is one thing for certain: we don't know anything.

The amount of knowledge and information in this world is far beyond the grasp of any person to ever obtain. No individual, not even a genius, could learn everything necessary to never make a mistake and always be correct in every decision.

You realize that wisdom is not a step by step guide to your destination, but a piece to the puzzle called life that helps you get a little closer to the bigger picture.

The legendary Nipsey Hussle once said, "The best teacher in life is your own experience."

You will have circumstances that you could not have seen coming. There will be times where you choose not to rely on your own wisdom and you make certain decisions. The key is not to harp on them but understand that you will never be perfect.

No amount of knowledge or spectating will give you all the answers.

Sometimes, the best thing life can do for you is put you through hell. Pain can be your best lesson.

Only a foolish person would ever believe they had all the answers. Only a foolish person would consider themselves wise because a wise person knows that they themselves know nothing in the big picture.

The little bit of wisdom we can gain in our life would be insignificant when compared to the amount of wisdom that is available in the world.

Therefore you do not need to stress yourself on being perfect in order to be wise.

You simply need to take the information available to you, watch others' experiences, and make the best decision you can, based on what you know.

The Bible reads in the 3rd chapter of Ecclesiastes, "To everything there is a season, and a time to every purpose under heaven. A time to be born, and a time to die; a time to plant, and a time to pluck up that which is planted. A time to kill, and a time to heal; a time to break down, and a time to build up"

It goes on for paragraphs detailing the ins and outs of life to reveal one unanimous truth: life is unpredictable.

There will be seasons where you will do everything right and still be wrong.

Seasons where you have picked everyone else up only to have the weight of the world fall back on your shoulders.

Seasons where you have fought for your relationship to work only for more heartbreak to follow.

Seasons where you work your ass off and still come up short of your goal.

If we try to fight these seasons too much they become bigger situations than they deserve.

Wisdom can provide you peace when you realize that every season comes to an end. They will never last forever.

Where you are losing today, you will win tomorrow. So stop trying to control every outcome. That is not wise. Learn to let things go and let life work its magic.

Embrace the beauty of struggle.

You will be happy and you will be sad. Mad and angry, then calm and peaceful. They all come in seasons. Ebbs and flows of the waves.

They say the worst thing you can do if you fall in deep water and cannot swim is to fight the waves. Yet the foolish man believes his flailing will somehow empower his situation and save his life. Only for him to quickly realize that he has hastened his own destruction.

Wisdom screams for you to remain calm. To lay on your back and let your body naturally float with minimal effort.

The more we fight the unpredictable and inevitable truths of life, the more we destroy ourselves. The fool believes he can control life enough to understand and win all situations.

The wise will release themselves from the weight of fighting life and will instead choose to float.

Life is like the ocean, and we as individuals are the boat.

We are powerless to the tide and a victim to the storm and its winds. Instead of fighting the ocean simply to lose like a fool. We would be wise to shift our sails in whatever direction the ocean wishes to take us at the time.

Letting go of the control we believe we have. Allowing life to happen with us rather than to us. Flowing our way to peace and fulfillment.

CHAPTER 9

STARTING & FINISHING

"Reach for the stars and if you don't grab
them, at least you land on top of the world"
- Jesse Paredes

One of the toughest things to do in this life is to start and finish. I know, it seems simple enough in its purest form. However, when you start to experience the different pushes and pulls of life, it starts to become far more difficult to complete our goals than it seems. You go through the constant changes of emotions that can hit you at different times. These emotions can either give you the energy and vigor to go after your goals or completely take away the motivation you had to make progress. This can create a state of being where we are stagnant. Full of potential, but empty of hope. It is in these moments that we must dig deep into our fears in order to make our dreams reality.

One universal fear we all share in life is never accomplishing the goals we want to obtain the most. The concept of failure has become so taboo that we run away from it completely rather than take the time to understand what it truly is. **To fail is not an adjective for who you are as a person. Failure is an opportunity. In fact, failure is a mandatory step on your pathway to success.** However, for most of us, we have never become comfortable with the idea of losing and so we are not prepared for the concept of true victory. We are afraid to lose and therefore lack the vision, belief, and courage it takes to win. This fear of failure can almost become paralyzing. Giving us so much anxiety over what could possibly happen in the future, or what has happened in the past, that we never take the steps to win in our present.

"Reach for the stars and if you don't grab them, at least you land on top of the world." This quote can be an excellent catalyst for people who are in the process of achieving their success and ready to take the leap of faith. However, have you ever thought about what happens to those who never let their feet leave the ground? Those people who are so comfortable in the mediocre level of life they walk in that they never do one courageous thing in all their days. It's not that these people did not have dreams and hopes for the future. The truth is, they simply were so fearful of the idea of failure that they never allowed themselves to take the first step in starting their journey to success. They live and they die. Literally, that is all. There is no legacy to be continued or generational wealth to be provided. Being comfortable in mediocrity is a dark place to lay your head.

The reality is, we all are not too far from being that exact person. I'm sure we all can recall plenty of times in life that we had the opportunity to go after something we really wanted but allowed the fear of the unknown to prevent us from taking the first step to start. Honestly, it is understandable to sometimes feel stuck in life and wonder what the right direction to go is. The problem, however, is not in feeling stuck, it is in believing you have no way to get out. **Once you fall into the trap of feeling incapable of progress and unworthy of opportunity, you have sealed your fate.** The only way out of this box is to change your mentality that redefines what the very essence of failure is.

Most people believe the word "fail" to be a death sentence that means the end of a journey. However, life has given us all the proof that failure is the exact opposite. When you fail a test, does the teacher decide you are no longer worthy of their lessons and give up? When you fail in a relationship, are you automatically deemed to be unfit for love for the rest of your life? The answer to both scenarios is clearly no. You can always try again and continue to strive for success. Society has told us a lie that when you lose, you will never win again.

Therefore, failure has become a mental state of being instead of a temporary assessment. To fail means it is your "First Attempt In Learning." Failure is not an endpoint, it is the catalyst to a new beginning. A jumpstart to opportunities that you are now more educated and prepared to receive. That dark cloud that gets you down can be removed simply by changing your perspective on how you view failure. By redefining how we view failure, we take control back into our own lives. By changing our minds, we have restored hope that not only is it worth it to start our goals, but it is even worth believing that we will finish and win.

The key to starting and finishing is to learn and apply a process that makes your steps to success easier and more tangible. To break a big goal down into many small goals, and make seemingly unimaginable heights far more obtainable.

J. Cole wrote, "If you ain't aim too high, then you aimed too low."

I like to think of goals in life like mountains, and us as the mountain climber. If you have ever watched a documentary of people who scale Mt. Everest, you will see one common practice in all of them: milestones. Nobody reaches the peak of the mountain in a day nor do they try to. They realize two very important things. **First: the greatest goals and feats in our lives never happen overnight.** They take time and dedication and perseverance. The second thing they realize is that it is necessary to have milestones on your journey to success. These milestones serve as guides to keep you on track towards your goal and provide time for reflection, rest, and improvement. While none of these milestones individually are as big as the overall goal, when put together they serve as a tangible and conceivable route to reach that mountain top.

Our goals in life are each a different mountain with its own peaks. Many of us struggle with starting and finishing these goals because we never made a realistic plan for success. If a random person wakes up and says

MYLES "THE MILLENNIAL" HARRIS

I am going to climb Mt. Everest today, they will almost certainly fail. They had no prior training, conditioning, or mindset for the journey they were trying to embark on. They set themselves up to fail. Far too often, we are the same way. We conceive an idea that we are passionate about, and instead of taking the time to set us up for success, we run unprepared into a battlefield. Then when we receive the inevitable set back that we self-induced, we lose that vigor and confidence that we previously had to achieve our dreams. Thus, never allowing us to finish our goals.

Experienced climbers spend years building the muscle memory and mental fortitude to defeat a climb such as Everest. They surface countless ranges in different environments and terrains so that they are battle-tested and prepared for whatever their next journey may throw them. The way they prepare for their goals is no different than how we must prepare for our own. We must take the time to meticulously think and develop a plan for success. There must be small and big milestones included in this plan that help to bring our dreams into reality. If we embark on a route that is based on tangible gains and wins, then no matter what the final outcome is we will be far better from it. **Abilities and talents will be revealed to us along a tangible journey to success that would not have been realized otherwise.** The motivation from continuously reaching your small targets will provide us with the necessary fuel to achieve our biggest goals.

There is no dream that is too far out of reach for the human mind. In every aspect of our life, if we want something, we must set ourselves up for success, not failure in order to achieve it.

We are conquerors and victors on this earth. **No longer do we sit around and allow our inability to prepare to be the inhibitor that prevents our dreams.** Every last one of you that has read this book to this point has accomplished something incredible. You used preparation by allocating time in your day to pick up this book to improve your personal mindset. You set tangible goals going page by page, and chapter by chapter that have allowed you to finish a piece of literature that I hope has improved your life. Through these thoughts, you now have the wisdom to take on any challenge live throws at you because you are prepared and battle-tested. Go out and reach for the stars in your life, and if you don't grab them at least you land on top of the world.

Always remember: Change your mind, change your life.

CPSIA information can be obtained
at www.ICGtesting.com
Printed in the USA
LVHW081121061120
670878LV00004B/15